The ARTS

THEATER

Howard Loxton

STECK-VAUGHN
LIBRARY
Austin · Texas

The Arts

Architecture
Dance
Design
Literature
The Movies
Music
Painting and Sculpture
Photography
Theater

Cover illustration: The phantom in The Phantom of the Opera, a popular modern musical that played to standing room only crowds in London, before it was transported to New York, where it enjoys continued success.

Series and Book Editor: Rosemary Ashley
Designer: David Armitage
Consultant: Trevor Griffiths Ph.D.
Chair of Department of Language and Literature,
Polytechnic of North London.
American Consultants: John and Sylvia Breckenridge,
JCB Theatrical Consulting

**Published in the United States in 1990 by
Steck-Vaughn Co., Austin, Texas,**
a subsidiary of National Education Corporation

First published in 1989 by
Wayland (Publishers) Limited

© Copyright 1989 Wayland (Publishers) Ltd.

Typeset at DP Press, Sevenoaks, England.
Printed in Italy
Bound in the United States.

2 3 4 5 6 7 8 9 0 Sa 95 94 93 92 91

Library of Congress Cataloging-in-Publication Data

Loxton, Howard.
  Theater / Howard Loxton.
    p. cm.—(The Arts)
  Bibliography: p.
  Includes index.
  Summary: An overview of theater as an art form with emphasis on the English-speaking theater. Includes information on the history of the theater, acting methods, staging, putting on a play, and theater careers.
  ISBN 0–8114–2359–X
  1. Theater—Juvenile literature. [1. Theater.] I. Title. II. Series: Arts (Austin, Tex.)
PN2037.L75 1990
792—dc20   89–11533
                                              CIP
                                              AC

Contents

1 What is Theater?

Below *Punch and Judy are glove puppets, but there are many other kinds of puppets operated by strings (marionettes) or by rods. In both Greece and the Far East it is the shadows of the puppets that are seen, viewed as silhouettes on a screen.*

Theater – what does the word suggest to you? It is not just a building. It also refers to the whole idea of plays and other kinds of dramatic entertainment. Theater can mean many things; it can mean a special occasion, ranging from a Punch and Judy show to grand opera, or a comedy show to classical ballet.

Perhaps you picture a theater as a place with scenery on a stage set behind red velvet curtains and rows of people sitting in front watching. In this book you will find that there are many other kinds of theater buildings, but "theater" – the experience of watching drama – does not require a special playhouse. It can be created wherever there is a performer and an audience – on the street, in a garden, in the corner of a classroom – as effectively as in a comfortable auditorium.

Theater can rely entirely on the talent of the actor and the imagination of the audience – and that is when it is often at its most exciting. On the other hand, theater can be very elaborate, making use of music, dance, colorful costumes, fantastic settings, and amazing effects that require all the skills of engineers, electricians, and designers using lasers and computerized controls.

This book will take you behind the scenes to show the technical elements of theater, and will tell you something of the way in which an actor prepares for a role. It will look at different types of theater around the world and the types of plays, that you might see. There is not enough space to include ballet, opera, or the many different kinds of puppet shows, although they are all theater, too.

Plays can tell a story – amuse, frighten, enlighten us, make us think. Often they can do all of those things together. However, you could say the same of television and the cinema, so how does a stage play in the theater differ from a screenplay at the movies or on the TV? The difference is that in the theater you are there!

Being part of an audience creates a group feeling that can intensify your reactions. You can feel that in the cinema too, but you are still quite separate from the film. Of course, you can get excited, frightened

Below left *Andrew Lloyd Webber's* Cats, *based on the poems in T.S. Eliot's* Old Possum's Book of Practical Cats *is one of the world's most successful musicals. Entirely song and dance, with no dialogue scenes, its clever costumes and dazzling choreography emphasize the feline characters of its all-cat cast.*

Below *Another theatrical landmark was the British National Theatre's production of the* Oresteia, *a sequence of three plays written nearly 2,500 years ago. It is a story of murder, revenge, and purification. As always in ancient times, the women's parts were played by men and all wore masks, which proved very expressive in performance. Here Orestes is surrounded by the Furies, who hound him for retribution after he kills his mother in revenge for her murder of his father.*

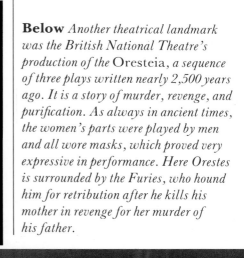

– annoyed even – but the film will go on just the same whether you are there or not and whatever your reaction to it. At a live (theater) performance your reaction is stronger, for each one of you is consciously using his or her imagination. There is also a two-way communication between you and the actors. No two theatrical performances will ever be exactly the same, whereas each showing of a film is identical.

Unlike films, the theater does not pretend to show you, for instance, the *actual* pyramids or the top of the World Trade Center. It rarely attempts to copy every detail of an actual scene, but the combination of the performance and your imagination can make its impact seem much more real than any film. For instance, it is unlikely that you are often startled when someone fires a pistol in a film or on television – but in the theater you almost certainly would be.

We do not know how theater began. Perhaps prehistoric peoples acted out thoughts and feelings before they had a word language for communication. Certainly early hunters had rituals when they dressed as animals, perhaps as a form of magic. In many folk cultures there are plays and dances that grew from ancient rites of symbolic sacrifice and rebirth. Ancient Egyptian Pharaohs played the role of the god Osiris in a ritual drama in which he was killed and then brought back to life.

In ancient Greece, theater began with the dances and songs performed by a chorus at religious festivals in honor of Dionysus, the god of wine and fertility. Actors are still sometimes called *thespians* after a priest called Thespis, who is credited with the idea of adding a solo performance to this chorus. This character, the first "actor" in

Right *Ritual and drama combine in the reenactment of a battle between the witch Rangda (at back of stage) and the benevolent Barong. This ritual dance drama has been performed for hundreds of years on the island of Bali.*

Right (inset) *An ivory carving of an actor in a tragedy, possibly Roman but showing the style of Greek theater from 200 BC, with a strongly modeled mask, high headdress, and thick-soled boots beneath the robe. The stumps below were once believed to be what the actors walked on but they are really just pegs to attach the figure to its base.*

Left *A Roman mosaic of about 200 BC, from Pompeii, shows actors getting ready for a* satyr *play. Seated is the poet, who both wrote and directed his play and was sometimes a leading actor, too. He is holding up the mask for the heroine. Next to it is the mask of the leader of the chorus, whose costume the man on the right is putting on. Center is the flute player who leads the music. Next to him an actor has his mask pushed up on his forehead.*

the modern sense, would exchange dialogue with the leader of the chorus of singing dancers. Later, other individual actors were added and dialogue between them developed.

The first plays took on the name *tragedies*, which in Greek meant goat-songs, perhaps because the chorus performed at the same time as a goat sacrifice was carried out, or because a goat was given as a prize to the best performer. Greek theater developed very rapidly and, by the fifth century BC, magnificent plays were being written that are still enjoyed today.

2 Theaters and Playhouses

Plays do not have to be presented in a special building. In ancient Greece performances first took place outside a temple or in the market square, before the huge hillside amphitheaters were constructed. These theaters had a circular dancing floor, known as the *orchestra*, with an altar at the center. Originally the audience stood or sat on the hillside. Later, wooden, then stone, seats were added. So too, was a structure behind the orchestra that gave actors an extra level on which to perform. Soon plays used three actors instead of just one. Each actor could appear in several roles by changing costumes and masks, but no scene made use of more than three main roles. The chorus, although reduced in number, remained important.

There were three types of play. Tragedies, always on serious subjects, were soon joined by short comic "satyr" plays (satyrs were the horse-tailed, goat-eared men who were supposed to be followers of

Far right *A French mystery play performance, of the martyrdom of St. Apollonia, painted about 1460. A circle of platforms are used for scenes (God in his heaven on the left), for musicians, and for spectators, who also stand or sit on the ground. The rat's mouth (right) is the entrance to hell.*

Below *The great theater at Epidauros, in southern Greece, dates from about 340 BC. It seats 14,000 spectators and is still used for drama festivals. The acoustics are excellent and actors can be clearly heard right at the back.*

the god Dionysus). These plays were often obscene burlesques, or "take-offs," on mythological stories. They were performed after the tragedies in the play competitions at religious festivals. Then comedy was invented. Originally, comedy was mainly amusing plays that echoed topical issues and poked fun at politicians or recent fashions.

The Romans copied Greek style theaters and performed plays in much the same way, though they built a more elaborate structure across the back of the orchestra. Most Romans preferred chariot races and gladiator fights to tragedy, but they enjoyed laughing at comic acrobats and plays based on the scandalous love-life of the gods. That was quite acceptable for the old religions, but after AD 313, when Christianity became the official religion of the Roman Empire, Church leaders strongly disapproved of jokes made about it. At first, performers were refused Church membership, and then, in the sixth century AD, the Emperor Justinian ordered all theaters to be closed.

However, even after the fall of the Roman Empire, some kind of theater survived, as can be seen by the fact that the Church continued to issue edicts against mime performers.

In the tenth century AD it was the Church itself that "reinvented" theater, acting out incidents from the Bible as part of the religious ceremony. As the dramatic elements grew greater, elaborate settings

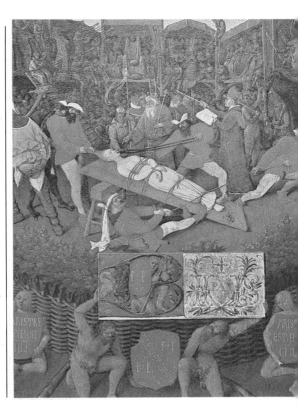

were sometimes built with clever effects, such as flying angels and twinkling stars, or devils entering the smoking mouth of hell. Plays were also performed outdoors, in front of the church or in the town square. Sometimes they were performed on a wide stage with scenes for individual episodes set up side-by-side, or ranged around the square. Elsewhere a ring of stages might be used, while in England and Spain individual scenes were often set up on carts which were pulled through the streets to allow each scene to be performed in turn at a number of locations. In Paris in 1420 the side-by-side staging was moved into a permanent indoor theater, establishing a style that was used for French plays for the following 200 years.

Fifteenth and sixteenth century interest in classical Greek and Roman culture drew attention to the surviving texts of Roman plays. Schools and universities began to perform them in their halls. In 1585 the *Teatro Olimpico* in Vicenza, Italy, was built as a re-creation of a classical theater, but roofed over and with the ceiling painted to look like the sky. Performances were lit by lamps and candles.

Traveling bands of actors, however, used only a simple platform stage which they would set up wherever convenient. They often made use of an inn yard or a small square for their performances, where spectators could watch from windows and balconies as well as from the ground. When Spain's first permanent public theater was opened, in Madrid in 1579, it was modeled on a closed-in yard or "corral". London's first playhouse, home base for the King's Men, the company that William Shakespeare became a member of, opened three years earlier. Called simply The Theater, it was galleried like an inn yard but circular, reflecting the shape of the bear and bull-baiting pits which drew crowds to watch these popular sports. The Globe,

Above *Traveling Commedia dell 'Arte players in Germany about 1730. This form of theater developed in Italy in the sixteenth century and spread through Europe. The actors had no script but improvised on basic plots and characters. Traditional characters, identified by their costume and a half-mask covering the eyes and nose, included Pantelone, the easily deceived old man; Capitano, the swaggering soldier; and cunning servants such as Harlequin, (second from left on stage). He has a wooden sword that makes a noise when he hits someone (giving us the word slapstick for knock-about comedy). There are also Punchinello (Punch) and a pair of lovers without masks. The Commedia may have links right back to the traveling players who survived the Church's ban on theater. This stage has wing flats and a backcloth like the indoor theaters of the time.*

Shakespeare's most famous theater, was built in the same style, on the south bank of the Thames River in 1599. Both Spanish and English theaters were open to the sky and performances were lit by daylight.

The actor-companies of Elizabethan England did not perform only in the London playhouses. They were also invited to put on plays for special occasions in the homes of the nobility, in the halls of the city lawyers, and for Queen Elizabeth herself. At Christmas they might be asked to provide entertainment for the royal festivities at Court. In summer, outbreaks of plague often forced theaters to close, then actors would tour the country, performing wherever they could get permission. At this time, most actors were male. Women were not normally allowed to appear on the stage.

For a time, from 1597, plays acted by boys from the London choir schools became very fashionable with audiences. Shakespeare pokes fun at them in the players' scenes in *Hamlet*. They performed in a so-called private indoor theater at Blackfriars. This was private to avoid the laws that governed the public theaters, but, although more expensive, anyone with the admission fee could attend. This theater, which was more fashionable than the Globe, was taken over by the King's Men, Shakespeare's company, giving them an indoor theater where audiences were protected from the many changes in English weather.

Above *The Swan Theatre, London, about 1596. This drawing is the only contemporary picture of an Elizabethan theater. A flag indicates there will be a performance that day. Below the flag a trumpeter calls the audience to the show. It cost one penny to stand on the ground, twopence to sit, and threepence for a cushion. Nobility might pay as much as twelve pence to sit in private areas.*

Left *The Teatro Olimpico in Venice. Behind the arches of the elaborate proscenium, or stage, wall are three-dimensional vistas of streets.*

Right (inset) *Sheridan's* A School for Scandal *at the Theatre Royal, Drury Lane, in 1777. Here Sir Peter Teazle discovers his young wife hiding behind a screen in another man's house. Note the forestage with its entrance doors overlapping audience boxes. The scenery is painted wing flats that slide on from the sides in grooves on the stage. The bookcase and window are painted on two large panels that meet in the middle. The shadow is painted, lighting is mainly by candelabra over the forestage which also illuminates the audience.*

Above *The Festival Theatre at Stratford, Ontario, in Canada, incorporates elements from both Greek and Elizabethan theaters.*

In 1642, stage plays in England were banned by the Puritan administration and all London playhouses were closed. When new ones opened in England after the restoration of the monarchy in 1660, they were all indoor theaters.

At the courts of Europe, especially in France and Italy, the aristocrats enjoyed their own amateur theatricals in the form of dances or ballets, called masques. These were more fashionable than plays, and were usually based on a mythological or allegorical theme. At first the participants simply entered wearing elaborate costumes and masks, to perform a dance. Songs, recitations, and dramatic episodes were added later, but, even with a full text and plot, they were intended mainly to give the maximum opportunity for display and effects. Famous artists, such as Leonardo dǎ Vinci, designed decor and machinery to create stage effects for them.

Such masques were performed in England, too. To please the court audience Shakespeare's play *The Tempest* includes a masque scene and many magical effects. One of the best-known English masque texts is *Comus*, by the poet John Milton (1608–74).

To suit this taste for spectacle, Italian revivals of Roman plays were now livened up by inserting *intermezzi* between the scenes. These consisted of songs, dances, and spectacles such as sea scenes with mermaids, or chases through a forest.

These dances and shows eventually developed separately into what we now call ballet and opera. Their effect on contemporary theater was to emphasize scenery and stage illusions at the expense of the text and the actor's skill. To create these effects, the central arch in the classical stage façade was enlarged and changeable painted scenery was added to the stage.

While an elaborate succession of scenery might be set up behind the stage arch, or proscenium arch as we call it today, most of the acting took place on the section of stage in front of it. This was the best place for the actors to be seen, lit by candelabra overhead or on the sides of the arch, and perhaps by a row of footlights at the front of the stage. Although Italian theaters developed tiers of lamps with reflectors to shine out from behind the scenery, it was not until the invention of gaslight and electric lamps in the nineteenth century that the actors fully retreated behind the arch, so that they appeared within a "picture-frame", which completely cut them off from the audience.

In the twentieth century, and especially in its second half, there has been a reaction against the "picture-frame" theater. Presenting older styles of play as though they were happening inside a box and the audience watching through an open side of this box, did not show the plays at their best. With film and television able to present audiences with passive photographic spectacle, people became more interested in effects that only theater can offer, and so there has been a return to the involvement of the audience with the actors, rather than a separation from them.

Theater architects and designers have looked back to earlier forms of theater and at the ways in which theater has developed in other parts of the world, and have drawn ideas from them. The audience today is often grouped around the stage, not just on one side of it. Sometimes the audience forms a complete circle. In theaters originally built with a proscenium arch, forestages have been built out into the audience to increase the contact with the actors. At one time a curtain always hid the stage when the audience entered the theater and descended between scenes or acts of the play. Often, today, you will find the curtain has disappeared altogether.

If you compare modern theaters with pictures of those from the past you will soon see similarities: the sweeping arc of the Greek theater, drawing the whole audience together; the projecting stage and galleries of the Elizabethan playhouse, bringing actor and audience closer. Most modern theaters have comfortable roomy seating and many older theaters often now seat only hundreds where thousands used to be crowded in. Some of the most interesting productions are given in small studio theaters or converted rooms where there has been no attempt to provide luxury seating. It has been suggested that audiences sitting back in comfortable seats may become passive viewers, whereas on harder benches, and without padded arm-rests to separate them from the people on either side, audiences are more unified, involved, and responsive.

Of course, there are still many theaters with proscenium arches, and for some kinds of show they may be best. Theaters of different shapes and sizes require different solutions to the challenges of putting on any particular play. Today spectacular effects and exciting surprises are as likely to happen right under your nose as on a stage some distance from your seat.

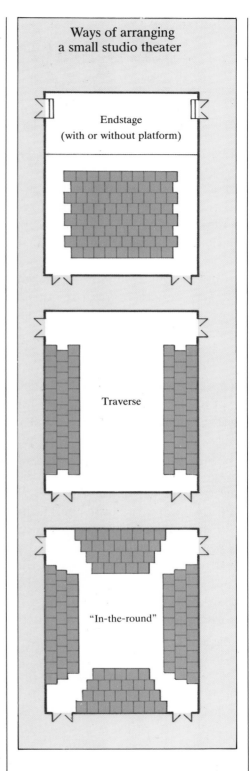

Ways of arranging
a small studio theater

Endstage
(with or without platform)

Traverse

"In-the-round"

Above *Some theater spaces are now planned so that the seating can be arranged to suit the particular production, or even be removed altogether so that the action takes place among the audience.*

Plays and Playwrights

The ancient Greeks saw tragedy, comedy, and satyr plays as distinct types. Such division into types, or *genres*, is useful in giving us some idea of what to expect when we go to the theater, though the distinctions are not so clear-cut today.

To the Greeks, tragedy meant something much more than a play with an unhappy ending. A tragedy presented the suffering and process of atonement of a hero, who was always someone of importance and fine personal qualities having to face the consequences of some previous action or decision. Its final resolution was usually positive, not sad. The philosopher Aristotle thought that the audience watching tragedy should experience a sense of emotional release called catharsis, the tragic events of the play "by means of fear and pity bringing about the purging of such emotions." People still argue about exactly what he meant.

The old (Greek) tragedies often showed human conflict with the gods. A later idea of tragedy was that it should show the downfall of a person through some personal failing or inability to deal with circumstances, for instance, Shakespeare's *Macbeth*. A modern tragedy might hinge on failure to cope with changes in society, such as the hero in Arthur Miller's *Death of a Salesman*. In all tragedy it is our own potential faults and failures that are at the center of the story.

Fifteenth- and sixteenth-century scholars who became interested in the ancient drama thought, quite wrongly, that tragedy had been written to strict rules, which they called the Three Unities: unity of time, place, and action. They thought that all the events in a play had to take place during the same day, ideally in the same time span as the performance, be at a single location, and present a single story with no sub-plots. This had a great influence on dramatists of the seventeenth and eighteenth centuries, especially in France. Plays on classical themes by the French dramatist Jean Racine (1639–99) are extreme examples of this form but even the topical comedies of his contemporary Molière (1622–73) show their influence.

No such rules constrained William Shakespeare (1564–1616), whose plays range as far and wide as his imagination and yours can take them. You will find comic scenes in the middle of Shakespeare's tragedies and moments of great seriousness in the funniest plays. There are plenty of fights and violent deaths as well. Despite their violent plots, ancient Greek plays never showed violence on the stage, perhaps because the theater was a kind of temple, but Shakespeare's plays and the "revenge-tragedies" of his near-contemporaries are very bloodthirsty indeed! For example, in Sophocles' play *Oedipus Rex*,

Right (inset) *Shakespeare's* Titus Andronicus. *A simple production in the Royal Shakespeare Company's bare studio theater creates color and excitement without elaborate scenery. At one time this play, with its many horrors – the Emperor Titus chops off his own hand, his daughter has her tongue ripped out and her hands cut off, and the villainess is made to eat her own sons baked in a pie – was rarely performed. Recently, there have been several exciting productions of the play.*

Right *Written in 1666, by the French dramatist, Molière* The Misanthrope, *is a high comedy, satirizing the artificiality of society; but it is also critical of its hero, who is obsessed with honesty and sincerity to the exclusion even of politeness. Molière's early farces were influenced by the Commedia dell' Arte and its stock characters. His comedies are still enormously enjoyable, not only for their wit but because Molière, himself a skilled performer, wrote marvelous parts for the actors.*

Oedipus blinds himself off-stage. In Shakespeare's *King Lear*, however, the character Gloucester is blinded in front of the audience.

Even further from the classical tradition was the emergence of a romantic kind of play. These included not just love stories and plays that allow the audience to escape into a never-never world, but plays in which characters are more like ordinary people.

From the end of the sixteenth century, dramatists such as Ben Jonson (1572–1637) began to write plays about merchants and shopkeepers, using a style of comedy that reflected contemporary behavior and fashionable society. These plays were very popular. Finest among this kind of comedy are the plays of Jonson himself, and, later, those of William Congreve (1670–1729), Richard Brinsley Sheridan (1751–1816), and Oscar Wilde (1854–1900), and some of the plays of Noel Coward (1899–1973). These are sometimes called "comedies of manners" because they deal with the way people behave in society.

Farce is another form of comedy. This is usually based on some kind of mistake that puts the characters into awkward and embarrassing situations. The characters are always recognizable types, the butts of the joke usually being people of some real, or imagined, social importance. Because the audience knows the situation is "a mistake" it is able to laugh at situations that might otherwise be upsetting – and there is a lot of pleasure in seeing pompous people get their come-uppance. *The Twin Menaechmi* by the Roman playwright Plautus (c 254–184 BC), *The Comedy of Errors* by Shakespeare, and the modern Rodgers and Hart musical *The Boys from Syracuse* are all farces which use the same plot from an early Greek play. Among the greatest farce writers have been the Frenchman Georges Feydeau (1862–1921) and

Left *A scene from Chekhov's* Uncle Vanya. *Constantin Stanislavsky (1863–1938) plays the part of Astrov (standing with hat) in this 1899 performance by the Moscow Art Theatre of which he was cofounder. Stanislavsky's theories on acting, based on an understanding of the motivation of the characters, has influenced actors ever since.*

the British playwrights Arthur Wing Pinero (1855–1934) and Ben Travers (1886–1980). French farces are usually saucily amorous but English ones nearly always manage (just) to avoid any improper sexual encounters!

Another genre, developed in the nineteenth century, is melodrama. This is a sensational theater of suspense and extremes: the hero is spotlessly good, the "bad guy" is a real villain, and the pure and innocent heroine is saved only at the last moment. Then there are plays in a style that the French call *Grand Guignol*, in which horror is piled on horror, and other dramas based on easily identifiable forms such as the detective story or thriller.

You will find a great many plays that cannot be categorized as a particular type, or that overlap several of them. But identification of a genre on the poster or other publicity material does give you some idea of the kind of experience to expect in the theater, and since each

Above *Carol Channing in the Broadway musical* Hello, Dolly! *(from Thornton Wilder's play* The Matchmaker*). The musical, once referred to as 'musical comedy', was usually little more than an excuse for presenting a number of unrelated songs. It has now developed into a much more dramatic show. Since* Oklahoma *(1943) which used the songs and dances to tell part of the story, musicals have dealt with all kinds of topics, from a killing (*Oklahoma*) to teenage gang rivalry (*West Side Story*) and the Crucifixion (*Jesus Christ, Superstar*).*

genre tends to demand a different kind of approach in the way the play is performed, it often takes only a few minutes of watching a play to know what style it is in – whether we are expected to find it funny, frightening, or whatever. Some people are more at ease when they know what is expected of them and they feel uncomfortable when a play combines different styles that make them laugh at the same time as dealing with a very serious subject. Others find that kind of play much more interesting.

In general, the staging of plays over the centuries has tried more and more to offer a "realistic" reproduction of the scenes they represented. By the middle of the nineteenth century a feeling was growing that the plays themselves should much more closely reflect the everyday world. Some writers set out to observe contemporary life in detail and to present its problems.

In 1875 the Norwegian dramatist Henrik Ibsen (1828–1906), who had previously looked to his country's history and legends for his stories, began to write a series of plays that investigated subjects such as individual social responsibility and the new expectations that women had for their lives. His characters speak naturalistically, although he presents some of his ideas in symbolic form. Many people found his plays shocking, especially *Ghosts*, which dealt with venereal disease (although it was never named as such in the play), but among his supporters was the Irish writer George Bernard Shaw (1856–1950). Shaw himself wrote many stylish and humorous plays which are full of lively discussion of political and personal morality. In Russia, Anton Chekhov (1860–1904) wrote naturalistic plays that mirrored the frustrations of middle-class life and the underlying revolutionary ferment in the latter days of Imperial Russia. Each of these playwrights examined the changing role of women that was beginning to take place.

The naturalism of Ibsen and Chekhov had a great effect on theater everywhere. Interestingly, their plays, though demanding great sincerity of the actors, are today frequently staged in very non-naturalistic settings without diminishing the realism with which they come across to the audience.

There have been, and are, many fine dramatists writing during the present century, some mainly to entertain, some to investigate political problems and injustices or explore emotional relationships. Some have written in verse, others have tried to copy real speech and behavior exactly, and some have deliberately adopted non-naturalist styles. One of the dramatists most influential on contemporary theater was the German Bertolt Brecht (1898–1956), who saw the theater as a place for argument, where the audience should not be encouraged to sit back and passively watch a play but should be kept in a state of constant critical awareness of the behavior of the characters and the ideas being presented. To do this he constructed his plays, for the production of which he was usually himself responsible, so that the audience was always aware they were in the theater. He interrupted

the plays with songs or comments flashed on screens.

Eugene O'Neill (1888–1953) is preeminent among American play-wrights. His passionate dramas range from very. naturalistic to broadly symbolic. Several reflect his Irish immigrant background, while *Mourning Becomes Electra* transplants the Greek story of Agamemnon to nineteenth-century New England.

One of the outstanding names in modern drama is Samuel Beckett (1906–), an Irishman who writes primarily in French. By writing plays that have no conventional plot but try instead to explore the very nature of existence, he again changed the expectation of what a play should be. Some find his works, such as *Waiting for Godot*, incomprehensible with their frequent silences and apparently illogical dialogues, but they are delicately constructed and can produce deep and resonant meaning for audiences who are prepared to make the effort to understand them.

Plays in the twentieth century may discuss political ideas, for instance those of Arthur Miller or Edward Bond. Or they may draw attention to injustices such as apartheid – a key issue for South African dramatist Athol Fugard. Alan Ayckbourne's plays make us laugh at the foibles of human nature; those of Tennessee Williams investi-gate personal anguish. Harold Pinter's intriguing dramas, like those of Samuel Beckett, expose the irrationality and uncertainty in human nature.

Above *The trial of Elizabeth Proctor (right) at Salem in Arthur Miller's* The Crucible. *This 1984 production by the Royal Shakespeare Company was a "promenade" performance, which means there is no fixed stage or acting area but actors and audience share the same territory for each scene, space being made when necessary. Here, tables have cleared a passageway for the actors, while the audience can sit or stand around them. This kind of staging brings actors and audience into the greatest possible contact, breaking down all barriers.*

4 Actors and Acting

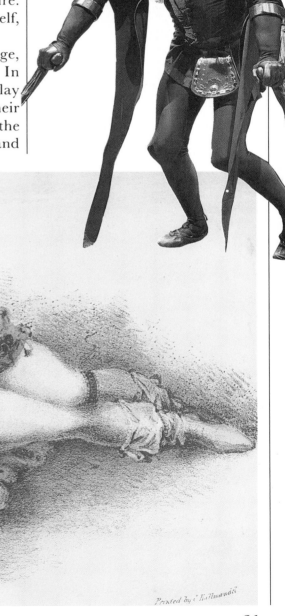

It is the actor's job to present the character in the play, whether it is Lady Macbeth or Peter Pan, or someone just like themselves. In some plays actors will be asked to make the audience think of them as real people behaving in an apparently natural way – though, of course, we will know they are acting and part of our pleasure comes from recognizing their skill. Some characters may be caricatures, to represent an idea or a type; for example, the wicked seducer in a Victorian melodrama or the grasping capitalist in a political satire. Here it is what the character stands for and not the character himself, that the audience must respond to.

Characters may stay entirely within the world created on the stage, or they may acknowledge the audience and speak to them directly. In each case they must find a way to convey to the audience what the play demands: to arouse their sympathy and involvement, appeal to their reason, sharpen their criticism, or even provoke their anger. At the same time they may be entrusted with speaking fine poetry and

Above *Sarah Bernhardt (1884–1923) as Napoleon's son in Edmond Rostand's* L'Aiglon. *This famous French actress often played men's roles, including Hamlet. She continued to act even after having a leg amputated. Plays were specially arranged so that she would not need to move around much.*

forming part of a pattern of shapes and movement which will have its own beauty.

We have all played games of "let's pretend", and acting is a little like that: you have to be able to imagine yourself in a different situation. In a game, however, you do not have an audience to convince and to keep interested, and to whom you must communicate through your acting. This demands great skill.

An actor needs three essential qualities: a voice that can be clearly heard and understood throughout the theater, a good memory to be word-perfect, and the ability to communicate with the audience. As well as moving and speaking to suggest the character, he or she may have to dance, sword-fight, make acrobatic leaps or dangerous falls, appear to play a musical instrument or work machinery – even to fly!

For a couple of hundred years people have argued as to whether acting requires the actor to experience the emotions of the character he or she is playing, or whether it is a matter of appearing to experience them, i.e., a matter of technique. Of course, the actor playing a murderer cannot *actually* kill his victim, but a fight can be made to look extremely violent without anyone being hurt. Some actors do claim to feel real anger or real grief when they act these emotions. Others claim they may actually be thinking about the meal they will have when the show is over.

You could divide actors in another way. The French have two words for them: *acteurs*, which means those who build the performance around their own personality, and *comédiens*, which does not mean comedians but character actors who create a person totally different from themselves. Of course, many actors are capable of both techniques, and all will draw upon their own experience when preparing a performance. Where something is beyond the range of what they have experienced (something as horrible as finding all their children dead, for instance) they may try to recall how they felt at the worst time in their lives, or search for some sound or gesture that seems to carry that kind of emotional pain. The English actor Laurence Olivier, when playing Oedipus, based his howl of anguish on the cry of a squirrel in a trap, because it was the most painful sound he knew.

Actors learn to notice the way other people and even animals move and behave so that they can recapture an image or an action when it fits a role. Remembering, for example, how an old woman hunched her back, or a gambling man slammed down his cards, could give an added reality to their acting.

Some actors will research the possible life of the character far beyond what the play tells them. If the setting is in the past they try to find out about the period. They might read about or even interview people whose lives seem similar to that of the character, to help them build their own image of the part. On other occasions actors will find the key to their performance in a piece of clothing or something belonging to the character: perhaps a smoker's big-bowled pipe, or a

Above *Laurence Olivier applies the finishing touches to his makeup for the role of Oedipus, at the Old Vic Theatre in 1946. Olivier is here enhancing his own features but he often used built-up noses and elaborate makeups for his characterizations.*

Inset *Makeup may be very light and subtle or bold and stylized. After applying an overall color as base this actor builds up a pattern of light strokes as highlights and deep red strokes as shadows, as he creates the role of Bumble in* Oliver, *Lionel Bart's musical version of Dicken's* Oliver Twist.

pair of spectacles that fits tightly on the nose and emphasizes short-sightedness, a string of pearls that they can fidget with, high heels or boots that fit too tight and change their walk, or a stutter or accent that the dramatist did not specify but that just seems right.

Our emotions and the ways in which our bodies react to them are not easy to separate, as you will know from occasions when you have tried to hide your feelings. By showing us the outward signs the actor can indicate to us a character's inner emotional state. An actor can often use the process in reverse. By carefully copying the physical signs, he or she can begin to create the feeling in themselves.

Try it yourself. Do it seriously or it will not work. What happens when you cry? Don't concentrate on the tears and wrinkling up your eyes. Think of the sniffs, gulps, and little sounds you make when you are trying to *stop* the tears. Start to make them and let them affect your breathing so that you find yourself gasping for air at the same time. Do you begin to feel uncomfortable and rather sad and sorry for yourself?

This kind of trick can be especially helpful in developing a performance in rehearsal. Having once created the emotional pattern, the actor can recall and reproduce it in performance. It can also be useful when an actor has to walk on to the stage already feeling an emotion strongly, instead of developing it in a scene within the play. Some actors can switch from themselves straight into the mood and character as they come in sight of the audience. But there are many stories of famous actors shaking a ladder (or the nearest supporting player!) behind the scenes, before they make a violent, angry entrance – and most of these stories are true.

While the dramatist provides the words and may give a lot of guidance to the actor in the script, it is the actor who must find a way of performing that reflects the character's situation and emotions. It may be necessary to tell a lie so that it is clear to the audience that it is a lie, but convincing to the other characters, or to sound very brave but let the audience know that you are terrified. The actor may have to convey information entirely through bodily movement.

Above *Paul Robeson (1898–1976), the American actor and singer, as Shakespeare's* Othello. *Many white actors have been successful in this challenging role and it is only recently that audiences have begun to accept black actors playing traditionally white characters.*

Right *Judi Dench in the title role of Brecht's* Mother Courage, *who drags her wagon across Europe following the armies of the Thirty Years War. Brecht's harrowing drama is a great challenge to actors and director, who must avoid attracting sentimental sympathy, so as to achieve the dramatist's aims.*

Above *French mime artist Marcel Marceau, seen here as Bip, his most famous creation. He was the first to attract modern popular audiences to wordless performances.*

Inset *Dan Leno (1860–1904), a famous English music hall artist and pantomime dame, as Widow Twankey in* Aladdin.

There are all sorts of signs and signals that people make without deliberately meaning to, and we soon learn to recognize them. You can easily see when someone is sad or happy, or perhaps even tell when they are feeling embarrassed. There are many tiny changes of expression or posture, many things that communicate information to us without us having consciously to think about them. An actor has to make sure that we notice them. In a large theater this means that they will have to be made clearer so that people farther away can see. This is one reason why actors wear makeup – to make it easier for the audience to see the expression on their faces. In the ancient Greek theater, actors wore exaggerated masks so that the audience could see at once what type of person they were. The mask also hid the actor's own face. Today stage makeup can do that, too, changing the actor's appearance by different color or shading, or adding false hair or even using putty to reshape a feature.

Clothes, too, will tell us a great deal about a character. Is he or she rich or poor, trendy or old-fashioned? The same things can have different meanings in different circumstances; we have to "read" them in the context of other information. Do dusty shoes mean that a man is lazy? – they could mean he has just been on a long journey. Sometimes clothing is like a badge. Most obvious are uniforms: this is a policeman, that a sailor, he's a general, she's a nurse, the man with a black tie and a black armband is in mourning. Those are all easy for you to recognize because they are "codes" you understand. If a play is set in a different period or a different country it may take a little longer to recognize, say, who is the captain of a spaceship, or the different meanings of two kinds of army uniform.

Oriental theater has a very rigid set of codes, developed for the theater and not necessarily drawn from life. A general in a Chinese opera, for instance, wears a set of flags sticking out from his shoulders to indicate his rank. For centuries *Nō* and *Kabuki* have been important forms of drama in Japan and in a *kabuki* play (a drama based on popular legends, in which male actors play all the roles) the actor's helpers may release the upper part of a character's costume so that its reverse becomes the lower part. The change is used to signify that the character has turned from a good into a bad person. Makeup and gestures, such as the positions in which a character holds a fan, can also have very precise meaning in oriental theater.

Although western theater sometimes borrows such techniques it is rarely as stylized or as formal as oriental theater.

How does one become an actor? Some acting is entirely instinctive, as can be seen in good child actors who can sometimes show amazing untrained talent. In the past, young actors simply learned from more experienced members of a company, but today most actors acquire the basic technical skills, and gain practice in interpretation and character development, by going to a drama school which specializes in training for the theater. Great actors, however, have a quality that cannot be learned: an ability to hold an audience and convince them against all odds that they are the character being portrayed.

Below *In the Japanese Kabuki theater there are only male actors. Specially trained performers,* onnagata, *play the female roles and because the performance depends on skill rather than appearance, a young girl may be played by a man several times her supposed age. Special stylized walks and gestures are used in particular circumstances and makeup can indicate character by its color.*

⑤ Behind the Scenes

The picture opposite shows a large proscenium-type theater with all the things that the audience does not usually see exposed to view: the wings, where everything is prepared ready to go on stage; the flies, where scenery and lighting are suspended on battens to be lowered into view; and some of the many people at work during a performance. Of course, not all theaters have a space above the stage for "flying" scenery. Instead, painted cloths may have to be rolled to enable them to be lowered from above, and, when the audience sits all around the stage, backstage will mean whatever place is used out of the audience's sight, while some of the mechanics may be well in view.

Many theaters have elevators – sections of the stage that can be raised or lowered, and traps – sections that can be opened to allow passage to and from the area below. If it is not possible to go below the stage then a pit or stairs down can be created only by building up the surface first with platforms. Platforms and steps are a frequent part of stage settings everywhere. A few stages can move from side to side so that a whole setting can be slid into view. Others have a turntable or revolve, which can be turned to show a series of different settings to the audience. Another way of bringing on a setting is to put it on a wheeled platform or "wagon", which is then rolled on the stage.

Although designers now use all kinds of materials for their scenery, including sheet metal, plastics, styrofoam, and fiberglass, most settings are still formed from flats and drops. A flat is a wooden frame covered with fabric or lightweight plywood. A drop is a large hanging cloth that is painted or dyed. Flats are light to carry and easily joined by rope lashings or loose-pin hinges and then supported by wooden braces (known as stage braces or stage jacks).

A vitally important part of any stage production is the lighting. Since the invention of gas and then electric lighting, it has been possible to control the intensity of lamps from a distance. Now there are a wide range of lamps with reflectors and lenses to concentrate or diffuse their beams. Colored plastic filters, known as gels because they used to be made of sheets of gelatine, change the light to the color required. A modern production may use hundreds of different lamps and have a very complicated succession of lighting changes (known as the lighting cues), though others will use the simplest means. The range of possible effects used to be limited by the skill of the electricians on their perch, just behind the proscenium arch, in manually operating switches and the handles of the dimmers that faded lights in and out. Today, many theaters have electronic controls operated by computer, which is operated from a booth at the rear of

Right *This drawing of a cut-away section of a proscenium-type theater shows the backstage areas and parts of the theater not normally exposed to the audience's view.*

28

A cut-out section of a theater

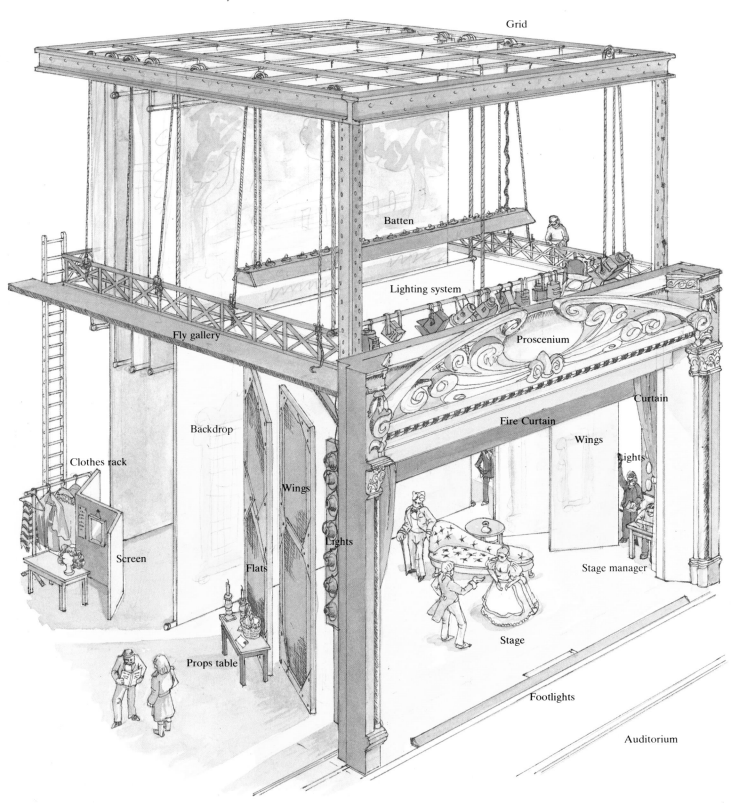

Fly loft

Grid

Batten

Lighting system

Fly gallery

Proscenium

Curtain

Fire Curtain

Wings

Backdrop

Lights

Clothes rack

Wings

Stage manager

Screen

Lights

Flats

Props table

Stage

Footlights

Auditorium

Schematic apparatus for flying

Compound drum

Flying wire

Theater grid

Lift control

Above *'Flying through the air with the greatest of ease' needs a skilled operator and practiced performers. For simple flights across or off the stage, vertical movement is provided by the operator; sideways movement is achieved by the pendulum effect of swinging on the wire.*

Right *J.M. Barrie's* Peter Pan *has the theater's best known flying scenes when Peter, Wendy, John, and Michael, with the help of a little magic dust, fly off to Never Never Land.*

the auditorium where the lighting controller can see the full stage. However, electricians are still needed on the stage itself, to handle portable lighting units, or connect and disconnect lamps as settings are put in place. They also need to check devices such as smoke effects, made by placing special chemicals on an electric heating element.

If voices need amplification, for a musical perhaps, a sound technician will mix and balance the fixed microphones and any radio-microphones worn by the singers. Taped music and effects and sound effects produced on the spot will probably be constructed and operated by the sound engineer. Dried peas rolled on the stretched surface of a drum can be made to produce a whole range of rain and sea effects; a shaken metal sheet can sound like thunder; a cylinder of wooden slats revolving against a piece of canvas can sound like wind. These traditional methods often sound more realistic than any recording of the "real thing".

During the running of the show everything is controlled by the stage manager who also follows the script, ready to give a reminder of lines on the rare occasions it is needed. The stage manager gives all the warnings and signals (known as cues) necessary to make sure that everything happens at exactly the right time. This is usually done using a system of green and red lights strategically placed in view of technicians or actors who may need to be told when to enter or commence an action if they cannot see on to the stage. Often a headphone system is also used to communicate with the technicians.

p. 25

PETER: Now, try; try from the bed. Just wriggle your
contd. shoulders this way, and then let go. ①

[The gallant Michael is first to let go, and is borne
across the room.]

MICHAEL [with a yell that should have disturbed Liza]: I
flewed!

[JOHN lets go, ~~and meets WENDY near the bathroom door
though they had both aimed in an opposite direction.~~]

WENDY: Oh, lovely!

JOHN ~~[tending to be upside-down]~~: How ripping!

MICHAEL ~~[playing whack on a chair]~~: I do like it!
WENDY FLIES

~~THE THREE~~: ~~Look at me, look at me! look at me!~~

[They are not nearly so elegant in the air as PETER,
but their heads have bumped the ceiling, and there is
nothing more delicious than that.]

JOHN [who can even go backwards]: I say, why shouldn't we go
out?

PETER: There are pirates.

JOHN: Pirates! ~~[He grabs his tall Sunday hat]~~ Let us go at
once! ②

[TINK does not like it. ~~She darts at their hair. From
down below in the street the lighted window must
present an unwonted spectacle: the shadows of
children revolving in the room like a merry-go-round.
This is perhaps what MR and MRS DARLING see as they
come hurrying home from the party, brought by NANA
who, you may be sure has broken her chain. PETER's
accomplice, the little star, has seen them coming,
and again the window blows open.~~]

PETER ~~[as if he heard the star whisper Come]~~: Right! ③ Now come! then. ④
All Together. Go!
~~[Breaking the circle he flies out of the window over
the trees of the square and over the house-tops, and
the others follow like a flight of birds. The broken-
hearted father and mother arrive just in time to get
a nip from TINK as she too sets out for the Never
Land.~~]

Second to the right, and straight on till
morning! [ALL FLY OFF STAGE LEFT]

NANA BARKS (off) Door opens. Mr + Mrs Darling
in doorway as lights fade.

---

p. 25

① Each flies in turn from
bed and back

W   P   M

J

② PP give Tinkerbell on
mantlepiece 'quiet' look

③ PP looks at others for
agreement. They nod

④ Indicates line up
behind him D-S.R.
John collects hat from
door.
W-M-J-PP
PP raises L. hand
Tink at window
Windows open

GO RED L Q
(Michael)

GO WHITE L Q
(John)

GO BLUE L Q
(Wendy)
GO Lx Q 53 (v. slow)
WARN GAUZE

GO Fx Q (Tink)
Lx Q 54

GO Fx Q (Tink)
GO Lx Q 54A
~~GO WINDOW~~
~~GO ALL LINES~~ when window
GO MUSIC open

GO Lx Q 55 (as they leave ground)

GO GAUZE
GO Lx Q 55A (BO)

In most proscenium theaters, the stage manager is usually located directly behind the proscenium arch. If the stage manager is on the audience's right, he/she is stage left as all directions are given from the actor's point of view. In Britain, the stage manager almost always sit stage left so this is called the PS (prompt side) and the other OP (opposite prompt). These names are used even when the stage manager is prompting from the other side. Theaters in continental Europe often had the prompter in a control box below the front of the stage, where he is still to be found in most opera houses.

As well as the stage-management team, a large theater will have a stage crew to handle scene changes and move furniture and properties. They must be as precise in their timing and placing as the actors themselves. Then there are all the people who make the costumes, the scenery and everything else that is not bought ready-made or borrowed for the play. This includes the dressers, who help the actors with their clothes, and the people who do the laundry, ironing, and any necessary repairs to costumes and scenery. This is quite separate from all those people who look after the audience and the theater building itself. It all adds up to a lot of people.

Above *Pages from the prompt copy for a production of* Peter Pan. *The prompt copy of the play is a record of what should happen, where the actors should be, and when sound effects are required. Each sound effects' "cue" is anticipated by a warning to the technicians or actors involved together with "calls" to the actors to make sure they are standing by to make their entrances. Warnings are usually marked in red, "goes" (instructions for cues) in green. A detailed plan will show the arrangement of furniture for each scene but a diagram of the relationship between furniture and actors may be all that is required to explain individual action.*

6 Shakespeare in the Theater

Below *David Garrick (1779–79) in the storm scene of* King Lear *at Drury Lane in 1760. Note that the actors are wearing the dress of their own time.*

There are many different kinds of play and they can all be presented in many different ways. Unlike a film, which will be the same each time you see it, a stage play is a living experience. Although an old film may still be very enjoyable, it is made for its own time; its attitudes and implications may no longer get a response from a modern audience. The theater is for its own time, too, but that time is today and each new production of a play presents it afresh. If aspects of an historical drama are no longer easily understood by a modern audience, it is up to the director to make them comprehensible.

Above *Anthony Hopkins as Lear and Seth Rohan as the Fool in the same scene from* King Lear *at Britain's National Theatre in 1986.*

32

Of course, the popularity of certain kinds of play or styles of production can be as much a matter of fashion as the clothes we wear or the way we decorate our homes, but directors rightly look for fresh and original ways to excite our attention. If they are reviving a play with which audiences are already familiar they will want to offer new insights to hold our interest. That is particularly true with the plays of William Shakespeare. The more popular ones may have been seen by the audience many times before, and most of us are familiar with some of the plays from studying them at school. That familiarity makes them ideal for showing just how differently they can be staged; how much one production of any play can differ from another.

When his plays were first presented by Shakespeare's own company, the stage was bare of scenery except for a few set pieces such as a tree or grassy bank. We know about these because we find them mentioned in property lists of the time. There would also be painted curtains and such essential furniture as a bed or royal throne. But this does not mean that the stage-picture was not exciting and glamorous. Luxurious clothes, waving banners, and shining armor added color and pageantry. Most characters wore the costume of Shakespeare's own time, with an occasional exotic touch, for example to suggest a Moor, a Roman, or a supernatural character.

Below *The graveyard scene in Hamlet performed in modern dress at the Royal Dramatic Theatre, Stockholm, 1987.*

Right *Oberon and Titania surrounded by their fairy band (represented by puppets) in a performance of* A Midsummer Night's Dream, *by the Royal Shakespeare Company in 1981.*

Below *A performance of* Much Ado About Nothing *on the thrust stage of the Shakespeare Festival Theater in New York's Central Park.*

It was not until the mid-eighteenth century that the actor-manager David Garrick began to introduce some attempt at historical accuracy into actors' costumes. By the late nineteenth century, audiences expected plays to be set and dressed to match their idea of the historical period in which they appeared to take place – even though Shakespeare had no knowledge of that period's style when he wrote them.

Although set designers had already made stylized and symbolic settings acceptable, audiences were shocked and excited when in 1923 Barry Jackson's Birmingham Repertory Theater reversed the process and began again to present Shakespeare in modern dress. Since then styles for Shakespeare have been very varied, from the exceptionally elaborate to the most simple. Their effectiveness is something only their audiences can judge in full.

7 Putting on a Play

When a play-producing management decides to put on a play it must first raise the money, or allot a budget from its resources. Commercial producers seek investors like any other business – theater people call them "angels" – but in many countries there are theaters that are not expected to make a profit. They are subsidized by national or local government, or by finding commercial and private sponsorship. Whether in the public or private sector, what happens in putting on a play is very similar from one situation to another, and even an amateur production will follow the same basic pattern.

If the play is by a living writer, or one who died within the period of copyright, permission must be obtained from the writer or agent before it can be presented, and royalty payments (fees for performance of the work) agreed on. Then a director must be chosen who is responsible for every detail of the way the play is presented. He or she will usually be involved in choosing a designer for the scenery and costumes (sometimes one for each and a lighting designer, too), appointing a stage manager, casting the actors, and commissioning music and choreography if needed.

Below *John Barton directing Shakespeare's* Titus Andronicus *with the Royal Shakespeare Company, halts rehearsals to discuss a problem of interpretation. The actors are already managing without the scripts. Notice the token props already on the table, including the pie which the Empress Tamora is about to eat before discovering her own sons are the filling. Actors not in this scene are sitting on the floor but still giving their attention to the discussion.*

Above *The empty stage of the Alhambra Theatre, Bradford, a typical gilt and plush proscenium theater ready for a new show to be set up.*

Right *An actress is fitted for her costume as Constance in a Stratford (England) production of* King John. *The dressmakers in the theater wardrobe have worked closely to the costume designer's designs, matching fabrics and cut to her specification. Costumes must not only fit comfortably and look good, expressing the character and the concept for the play; they must also enable the actor to make all the necessary moves without hindrance.*

Until near the end of the nineteenth century it was often the leading actor, or sometimes the author, who decided where to place the actors on the stage – usually simply as a background to the leading roles. A German duke, Georg II of Saxe-Meiningen, who had his own court theater, seems to have been the first to carefully control every detail of a production to produce an overall effect. In the twentieth century the director has become one of the most important people in the theater. The play to be performed may itself now be the choice of the director.

The director will study the play to understand what the dramatist is saying, and to discover its strengths and weaknesses. He or she will think about how the characters should be portrayed, the kind of settings and costumes needed, and the use of music. All these will be related to the facilities and finances, available. If it is a new play, changes may be discussed with the dramatist. With an old play the director may decide to leave out some passages – to make it shorter, either because the play seems easier to understand without them or to make it fit the resources available. To cut costs, some parts can be "doubled" (one actor playing more than one character), or minor characters removed and their words given to another.

The director will discuss ideas with the designer, who will then produce models for the settings, followed by detailed plans and drawings and designs for the costumes. The settings must change easily from scene to scene and if the play is to be presented in several theaters (for instance by a touring company) it must fit all the different stages and be easy to transport. If the production is to be very simple, or there is a very long time for rehearsal, it may be possible to put off design decisions to allow for ideas to develop during rehearsal.

The director chooses actors who will be able both to create the characters and be compatible with each other. Height and special skills must be considered as well as acting ability. The director may invite actors to audition for certain parts. Each will perform at least one passage to demonstrate their skill and, if they seem suitable, read one of the parts being cast. They may have to come back several times before the director makes a decision, and actors can attend hundreds of auditions and still not get a job.

Above *A rehearsal for* The Wizard of Oz *with the Tin Man, Dorothy, the Cowardly Lion, the Scarecrow, and Toto, for the Royal Shakespeare Company.*

Left *The same scene in performance.*

Rehearsals may be held on a stage or in any room big enough to match the floor area of the settings. They usually begin with a complete reading of the play and presentation of the designs. The director may discuss his or her approach to the play, and perhaps suggest books or other research that will help the actors to understand its background and the characters they will play.

For later rehearsals the positions of the scenery (set) are marked on the floor, ideally with portable steps and platforms if they use different levels, and any available furniture until something similar to the actual pieces is available. The director will work through the play, fixing positions and moves; this is usually known as "blocking" the play. With a short rehearsal period he or she may have worked these out in advance but will be ready to accommodate the actors' ideas into the pattern.

Scenes and parts of scenes will be gone through again and again to improve their presentation and develop the actors' performances. The director, unlike the actors, can take in the overall effect, and so will offer criticism and suggestions. When the actors can remember their lines their performances will become more fluent, picking up cues more rapidly and the director will be able to concentrate on more subtle details and improving the rhythms of the performance.

Above *The Royal Shakespeare Company rehearse the scene in which the court watch traveling players perform "The Mousetrap" in Shakespeare's* Hamlet. *The player king and queen wear their crowns, Ophelia and Queen Gertrude wear long skirts and several of the men wear coats or gowns to help them feel the correct movement of their costumes. Important features of the set have been marked out on the rehearsal floor with tape.*

38

Above *The costume design for* King John *at the Shakespeare Festival, Stratford, Connecticut.*

Below *Roger Rees rehearsing a sword fight in* Hamlet. *Sword fighting is only one of the accomplishments that actors need to master. Stage fights of all kinds must be performed exactly as planned if injury is to be avoided.*

A director will usually be very encouraging, but occasionally may deliberately create tension between the actors to spark off a reaction that will help them to find the key to making a scene work. He or she may ask them to improvise – to play the scene in their own words, or to free their imagination and give them a fresh approach. Some plays are developed entirely from improvisations based on the actors' ideas, with a dramatist perhaps called in only to write a final script.

All through rehearsals the stage management team follow all the rehearsals, prompting the actors with any words that they forget and making a note of every move and action in their copy of the script. This must always be kept up-to-date to include any changes that are decided. They will provide all the sound effects and list all the "props" that are needed for the play, from a handkerchief to a grand piano, and make sure that arrangements are made to obtain them. Meanwhile they will provide temporary substitutes for objects the actors will need to use or carry. Actors may also wear rehearsal substitutes for items of clothing that would affect the way they move – a crinoline for instance – so that they will not suddenly discover at the dress rehearsal that the costume changes their timing or the space they need.

To save actors from hanging around when they are not needed, the director and the stage management will draw up a schedule of when particular scenes will be rehearsed. One group of actors may work under an assistant director, or the stage manager, while others work with the director. There may be extra sessions with a music coach if actors need to sing, or with a choreographer for dances. When not needed for rehearsal, actors may be called to costume fittings or to buy clothes with the designer. They may need to have lessons in a new skill, such as magic tricks or some other speciality needed for the part, as well as learning their lines. Actors work long hours, especially when they are rehearsing one play during the day and performing another play at night.

After weeks of rehearsal the actors must now face the judgment of the audience on the other side of the footlights.

The last few rehearsals will attempt to run through whole acts without stopping, just as in performances. Only then will the play's timing and rhythms become clear. The stage manager uses a stopwatch to note how long each act takes. As soon as the theater is available – perhaps in the early hours of Monday morning after Sunday night's show has been dismantled – the technical staff set up the scenery, lighting, and other equipment. Hundreds of lamps may have to be carefully cabled, placed, and focused. Then, if time allows, a technical rehearsal follows in which the actors go through all their moves and cues, though without having to attempt a performance, so that all the changes, lighting, and effects can be tried and adjustments made. The actors will be in costume and makeup because these will affect lighting and maneuverability (will that wide skirt go through that narrow doorway?) and use the real props (watch out, that banner snags the scenery!). Then the actors go home to rest while the director, stage management, and technical crew try to solve the problems.

Now comes the dress rehearsal – a complete performance. With luck, nothing goes wrong, but if it does everyone tries to carry on. Theater superstition says a disastrous dress rehearsal is in fact good luck for the opening night, but everyone still prefers it to go well. Some companies will have more than one dress rehearsal, but many may finish only just in time to let the audience in to see the opening show. So it's keep your heads and "break a leg" – an odd phrase actors use to wish each other good luck!

⑧ Going to the Theater

A brilliant production is only part of the recipe for good theater. A play needs an audience, and that audience needs to be attracted to the theater and looked after when they are there. A theater requires people to sell tickets, show the audience to their seats, and help in many other ways. It must also check stocks of everything from food and drinks for its refreshment bars to toilet paper, as well as keeping everything clean and in good repair. There are strict regulations to ensure the public's safety and these must be rigidly followed.

The production company, or the theater management if they are their own producers, will put a lot of effort into publicity. There will be posters, handbills, and advertisements. The press officer will try to get as much information as possible about the production published in the press, and might also try to get the show mentioned on television and radio, both in advance of the opening night and while the show is running. Advertisements can be expensive, but press articles about the show may provide free publicity. Few theater companies can afford to buy advertising time on television, but mention of a play on a talk show, for example, will be heard by millions of viewers.

Tickets have to be printed and put on sale and programs prepared and ready for the opening night. Free tickets will be sent to newspaper and magazine critics who write reviews on new productions.

Above *Reserving a ticket in advance, at the office in the theater foyer. There may be several different ticket prices for a show, according to what part of the theater the seats are in – those with the best view are the most expensive.*

Left *Waiting to enter one of London's famous theaters, for a performance of the very successful* Phantom of the Opera, *with music by Andrew Lloyd Webber and lyrics by Charles Hart and Richard Stilgoe. It is a good idea to check the performance time in newspaper listings or with the theater if it is not printed on your ticket, and arrive with time to spare to find your seat. You may want to buy a program giving the name of the actor playing each character, the people responsible for the production and perhaps some background information about the play. They are usually on sale in the foyer or just inside the auditorium.*

41

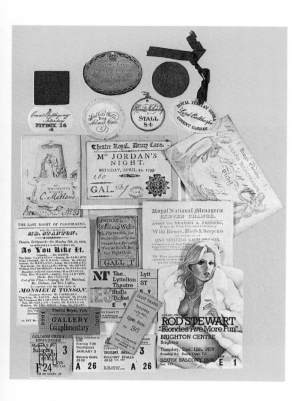

A collage of British theater tickets. Over the years these have taken many forms. The tokens at the top are metal and bone and were used in the eighteenth century by theatergoers who had paid for a regular seat. Others are more familiar types of ticket.

You can find out about which plays are being performed on a specific date by reading posters on buses or billboards, by picking up leaflets from the theater itself (where you might also find leaflets for other theaters, too), or by reading the advertisements and listings in the newspapers. Larger cities such as New York, Chicago, Atlanta, Houston, and Los Angeles, have magazines that cover all kinds of events and shows from discos to art exhibitions, and from theaters to political rallies. Usually, they list even the smallest theaters. Sometimes you can ask the theater to put your name on a mailing list by writing or phoning. You may also decide to take out a subscription to all the plays performed at a specific theater or by a repertory group or stock company. A subscription guarantees you a specific seat at all performances in the theater, and may also allow you to purchase additional seats at lower prices.

Having decided there is a play you want to see, you can either go to the theater to buy your tickets or reserve them by telephone. Unless you can charge the ticket to a credit card account you will have to collect a ticket reserved by telephone within a specified time. The theater cannot risk you not showing up to pay for it when they could have sold it to someone else. Tickets can also be bought from agencies who sell them for a range of theaters, rock concerts, and other entertainments. (They often have branches in large department stores. However, you usually have to pay an extra fee to them.)

If you go to the theater box office (usually a counter in the main lobby but sometimes in a separate building for advance reservations) you will be able to look at a plan to see exactly where the seats at each price are and the location of those that are still available. Of course, you can always turn up just before the performance to see if there are some seats still available. Even if all other seats are sold long before, some theaters hold back a few cheaper seats for sale on the day of the performance for people who cannot plan ahead. To obtain them often means lining up when the box office opens in the morning. If all the seats are sold you may be able to stand at the back of the theater. As a last resort you can hope for returns, tickets brought back by people for resale because they or their friends are not able to use them. This means lining up again before the performance time. Ask the box office staff what time lines are likely to form.

If you buy a reserved seat there will be a number on your ticket, usually with a letter to indicate the row, to show where you should sit. With an unreserved seat you sit in whatever seat is still available at that price, so early arrivals have first choice.

Do not be late for the performance. If you are, you may have to wait outside until there is a break so that you do not disturb the rest of the audience and the actors. Unless the play is less than an hour-and-a-half long there will almost certainly be an intermission. Shortly before "curtain up" (a term still used to describe the beginning of the performance even when no curtain is used) and before the end of the intermission, announcements will be made or bells rung when there are three minutes and then one minute to go, giving you time to get back to your seat.

The play may be very exciting and everyone may be laughing, even crying, but avoid chatting or rustling candy wrappers and try to suppress any coughs or sneezes. It is not like being at home in front of the television. All those things can be very distracting and annoying to both audience and actors, and spoil others' enjoyment of the show. In a musical or light comedy people will often burst into applause at some part of the performance they find particularly skillful or enjoyable, but in more serious plays this would interrupt the mood and concentration. People then wait until an intermission, or the end of the play, to show their appreciation.

Theater performances have their own codes and conventions for conveying information. It helps to know them, just as it helps to know the rules if you watch a game of football. Some you will already take for granted because they are part of ordinary life; others will have been familiar to you since childhood, such as miming, i.e., going through the actions of using, say, imaginary cups and saucers to drink coffee. Sometimes a production will create its own conventions, but you can pick them up very quickly once you know the kind of thing that happens. You already do the same when you are watching television, even if you do not realize it! So get on with enjoying the play.

This book has shown you a little of how theater is created and how easy it is to enjoy, but no book can convey the excitement of a performance, not even the anticipation of waiting for it to begin. To share the magical experience of live theater you must go to a play yourself.

Below *The curtain call for Stephen Sondheim's musical* A Little Night Music. *The show is over and members of the cast receive the audience's applause.*

So You Want to Be an Actor or Work in the Theater

Many schools present plays and there will probably be at least one amateur dramatic society in your town or area. Sometimes these local drama societies, often called civic theaters, employ professional directors to help them put on plays. They certainly are excellent opportunities for young people to learn everything that is required when a play or musical comedy is performed.

In any case, you should think very hard before deciding to embark on a career in the theater. Many actors spend much of their lives out of work and wages are low except for the very famous. The unemployment rate for professional actors is probably around 80%. There are many other jobs in theaters, both in technical and administrative departments, but there is a lot of competition for these also. You have to be very good, very determined, and very lucky to be successful.

In addition, most professionals find that they must join a union to be employed in certain American cities. For example, all Broadway theaters in New York, and most major regional and touring productions use members of the unions exclusively. The professional stage actors union is Actors Equity Association (AEA) and the professional stagehands union is International Alliance of Theatrical Stage Employees (IATSE).

There are many private, fee-paying specialist drama schools for professional training and most actors enter the profession through them. Most actors also spend some time in a college or university program and then study with special coaches. Most designers now entering the business have graduate school degrees (MFA). As for technicians, some have college degrees but many learn the trade through their families or through apprenticeship programs run by local unions.

Many people feel it is wisest to qualify in some other professional area first before starting drama training. If you do this you will always have the qualifications to fall back on another career if you turn out not to be one of the lucky ones who manage to find work in the theater.

Your school career counselor will be able to provide you with information on drama courses and schools and the qualifications needed for them. In addition, he/she will help you find books and pamphlets on other careers in the theater and related fields.

Further Reading

General theater history
History of the Theatre by OSCAR BROCKETT (Allyn and Bacon, 1977).

About being an actor
Actor and His Body by LITZ PISK (Theatre Arts, 1976).
An Actor's Ways and Means by MICHAEL REDGRAVE (Theatre Arts, 1979).
On Acting by LAURENCE OLIVIER (Touchstone/Simon and Schuster, 1987).
Early Stages: The Professional Theater & the Young Actor by WALTER WILLIAMSON (Walker & Co., 1986).

Putting on a play
A Stage Crew Handbook by SOL CORNBERG and EMANUEL GEBAUER (Harper and Row, 1957).
Stage Crafts by CHRIS HOGGETT (St. Martin's Press, 1977).

Scene Design and Stage Lighting by OREN PARKER and HARVEY SMITH (Holt, Rinehart, and Winston, 1974).
Scenery for the Theatre by HAROLD BURRIS-MEYER and EDWARD COLE (Little, Brown and Co., 1971).

Plays
You will generally find scripts of plays in library card catalogs under Drama or Literature, and under the playwright's name. Many have also been published in paperback.

Magazines/Newspapers
Two general magazines or newspapers that you will find in most libraries and some newstands are *Variety*, the theater trade journal, and *Theatre Crafts*, which is more technical.

Glossary

Act Sequences of scenes in a play which are played without an interval.

Allegorical In which the apparent meaning of characters and events in a play is used to symbolize a deeper moral or spiritual meaning.

Atonement The act of making amends for a crime or wrongdoing.

Audition A trial performance given by an actor applying for a part in a play.

Auditorium The audience area at a theater – also known as the "house".

Backdrop A large painted canvas that hangs at the back of a stage set.

Blocking Fixing actors' movements in rehearsal and entering them in the prompt copy.

Burlesque A play that parodies or caricatures someone or something in a ludicrous way.

Choreographer The composer of dance steps or sequences for ballet and stage dancing.

Chorus In classical Greek drama a lyric poem sung by a group of singing dancers (originally as a religious rite), or the actors who sing the poem and comment on the action of the play.

Comedy A play that looks humorously at human character and behavior, usually including amusing incidents.

Cue Words or actions to which an actor answers; the term is also used to mean the moment for a change of effect, scene, or lighting.

Director The person who rehearses the actors in their roles and decides and coordinates the artistic aspects of a production.

Dress rehearsal A final rehearsal, with full scenery, costumes and effects.

Effects Any sounds, special lighting devices, etc., which are required by the play.

Farce A funny play, in which characters usually represent basic types and in which the action relies on mishap, coincidence, embarrassing disclosures, and visual jokes.

Flat A scenic unit consisting of a wooden frame. It may have an opening in it to take a door, window, or fireplace.

Flyloft The space above the stage where lights and scenery can be hung out of audience view.

Footlights Lights at the front of the stage that shine upward. They were originally needed to counteract strong shadows from lamps hung overhead but are now rarely used.

Genre Category or style, referring especially to an artistic work.

Improvise To depart from a script, or work without one, with the actors inventing their own lines.

Lift A section of stage that can be raised or lowered.

Mask A covering worn to hide the actor's face or to represent a different face. The word also means to hide things from the audience, such as equipment and backstage areas, or one actor blocking the audience's view of another on stage.

Masque A spectacular dramatic entertainment, involving dances. These were popular among nobility in the sixteenth and seventeenth centuries.

Melodrama A sensational romantic drama portraying extremes of character.

Orchestra The circular dancing floor in ancient Greek theater, where most of a play took place. From a Greek word meaning "to dance".

Producer The person or company who presents the show, raises the money, and employs the cast and production team. Until the 1960s the word was used for what is now called the director. The producer was then known as the manager.

Prompt A reminder of lines that an actor has forgotten, given by the prompter (usually the stage manager) or sometimes by another actor.

Prompt copy (or prompt book) Copy of script in which positions and moves of scenery, furniture, and actors and all cues for changes and effects are recorded.

Prop(erty) Anything used on the stage that does not form part of the scenery, costumes, or technical equipment, e.g., food, drink, or items carried or used by the actors.

Proscenium Originally a shallow platform in Greek theater. Now the wall dividing the auditorium from the stage, into which is cut the proscenium arch through which spectators view the action.

Rehearsal The practicing and development of a play.

Repertory company A theatrical company that performs a collection of plays for public performance, usually at its own theater (also known as a stock company).

Royalty The percentage of income from ticket sales paid to a playwright, designer, composer, or other person instead of, or in addition to, a wage.

Stage manager The person responsible for organizing rehearsals, coordinating technical departments, making and updating the prompt script (with positions, moves of scenery, etc.), and running performances.

Theater-in-the-round A theater with the audience on all sides of the acting area.

Thrust stage A stage that projects into the audience.

Tragedy Serious drama in which the main character is overcome because of a personal failing or social and psychological circumstances.

Trap A section of the stage floor that can open to form a grave, or allow access to and from below the stage.

Traverse staging A rectangular acting area with the audience on both of its long sides.

Turntable The circular area of a stage that can turn, revealing a new set of scenery.

Wings Areas backstage at the side of the acting area. Also flats or curtains hung facing the audience at the sides of the stage.

Wardrobe Costumes and the staff and premises that handle them.

Picture Acknowledgments

J. Allan Cash 4 (top), 7 (top), 36 (top), 41 (lower); Channel 4 Studios 5 (lower); Donald Cooper 4–5, 19 (both), 20, 23 (top), 24 (lower), 26, 30, 34 (top), 37 (lower), 39 (lower), 40; David Cumming 41 (top); Mary Evans 11 (top), 15 (lower), 21 (lower), 25 (lower), 28; Howard Loxton 31, 33 (inset), 34 (lower), 39 (top); Mander and Mitchison 22, Mansell 32 (top); National Theatre/Donald Cooper 32 (inset), 33 (lower); Photri 17, 23 (inset), 24 (top), 43; Popperfoto 23, 36 (lower); Royal Shakespeare Company 15 (top), 24, 35, 37 (top), 38; Ronald Sheridan 6, 8–9; Theatre Museum 42; Topham Picture Library 18, 23 (top), 25 (top), 34 (both), 39 (top); Victoria and Albert Museum 42; Wayland Picture Library 9 (top), 10, 11 (lower), 12 (top), 15 (top), 16, 21 (top), 27. Diagrams on pages 13, 29, 30 are by Malcolm Walker. Cover picture © Clive Barda/Woodfin Camp Associates.

Index

48